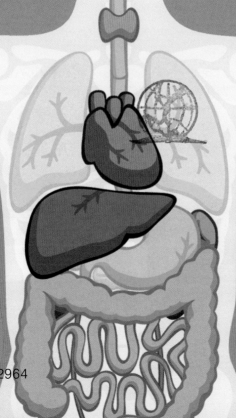

Chomp and Chew, to a Healthy You!

**Molly Carroll
and Kelli Hicks**

Rourke
Publishing LLC
Vero Beach, Florida 32964

www.rourkepublishing.com

PHOTO CREDITS: © Monika Adamczyk: Cover; © Nathan Shelton: Title Page; © Damon Taylor: All Illustrations; © Olga Solovei: page 5; Julián Rovagnati: page 7; © Nicole S. Young: page 9; © Justin Horrocks: page 11; © Joannawnuk: page 13; © Renee Brady: page 15; © Suprijono Suharjoto: page 17; © Andrea Gingerich: page 19; © Courtney Weittenhiller: page 21; © morganl: page 23 top; © Andi Berger: page 23 bottom; © Quavondo Nguyen: page 22 top

Editor: Jeanne Sturm

Cover design by: Nicola Stratford

Interior design by: Tara Raymo

Library of Congress Cataloging-in-Publication Data

Carroll, Molly.
  Chomp and chew to a healthy you / Molly Carroll and Kelli L. Hicks.
     p. cm. -- (My first science library)
  ISBN 978-1-60472-541-4
  1. Children--Health and hygiene--Juvenile literature. 2. Children--Nutrition--Juvenile literature. I. Hicks, Kelli L. II. Title.
  RA777.C33 2009
  613'.0432--dc22
                                        2008025160

Printed in the USA

CG/CG

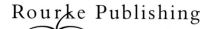

Rourke Publishing

www.rourkepublishing.com – rourke@rourkepublishing.com
Post Office Box 3328, Vero Beach, FL 32964

How can you grow tall and strong like me?

Feed your body healthy foods.

5

Drink milk for strong bones and teeth.

Eat fruits and veggies everyday.

9

Don't forget to chomp and chew!

It helps your food go down SMOOOOth.

12

13

Drink lots of water every day.

Get hot and sweaty when you play.

Give your body time to rest.

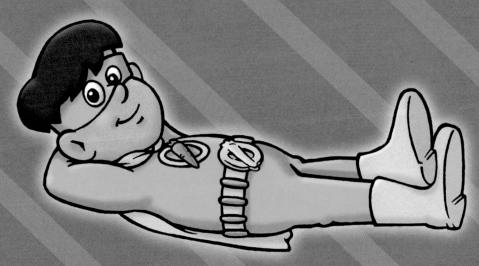

19

These are the things that make a healthy YOU!

Glossary

body (BOHD-ee): All the parts that make up a person or animal is a body. The human body is made up of a head, neck, torso, two arms and two legs. The adult body has 600 muscles.

bones (BOHNZ): Bones are the hard, white parts that make up the skeleton of a person or an animal. The adult body has 206 bones. A baby's body has 300 bones. Some of them fuse together as the baby grows.

fruits (FROOTS): Fruits are the fleshy, juicy products of plants that contain one or more seeds and are usually edible. Bananas grow in a large bunch from the point where the leaves attach to the stem of the plant. Eating fruit every day can help to keep your body healthy.

teeth (TEETH): Teeth are the white, bony parts of the mouth that are used for biting and chewing food. Adults have 32 teeth. Teeth can help you to speak clearly.

Index

Further Reading

Figtree, Dale. *Eat Smarter: The Smarter Choice for Healthier Kids*. New Win Publishing, 2006.

Kleinberg, Leigh, and Yee. *Grover's Guide to Good Eating (Happy Healthy Monsters)*. Random House,Inc., 2007.

April, Ryan, and Iverson. *We Like to Move: Exercise is Fun.* Hohm Press, 2007.

Websites

www.jhucct.com/nash/open/resource/wellpoint.pdf

www.sesameworkshop.org/healthyhabits/

www.foodplay.com

About the Authors

Molly Carroll loves visiting her local farmers' market to see what foods are in season.

Kelli Hicks lives in sunny Florida with her husband and daughter. They enjoy soccer, skating, and riding bikes. Their favorite fruits are bananas, watermelon, and pineapple.